one whole day

WILD PONIES

BY JIM ARNOSKY

NATIONAL GEOGRAPHIC SOCIETY

Washington, D.C.

On Assateague Island
out in the sea,
there's a small herd of ponies
living wild and free.

It's a colorful herd
with one white and black
and one chocolate brown
with white spots on its back.

On Assateague Island
out in the sea,
each day is exactly
the way it should be.

In the morning they walk
from the beach to the dune,
where they graze on the grasses
and sea oats till noon.
Then they follow the stallion
as he leads the way,
through the muck of the mudflats
to a marsh by the bay.

On Assateague Island
out in the sea,
a mare tends her foal
in the shade of a tree.

Mother and foal
join the herd in the sun.
Soon they're all having
some wild pony fun.

On Assateague Island
out in the sea,
there's a foal and a fawn
playing hide-and-seek.

Pony tails swoosh
at mosquitoes and flies.
The tide flowing in
makes the marsh water rise.

On Assateague Island
out in the sea,
each ending day
floats away on a breeze.

Back at the dunes
as the sun's going down,
the foal sees the ocean
and hears the surf pound.
She runs to the water
to see how it feels,
and whinnies and prances
and kicks up her heels.

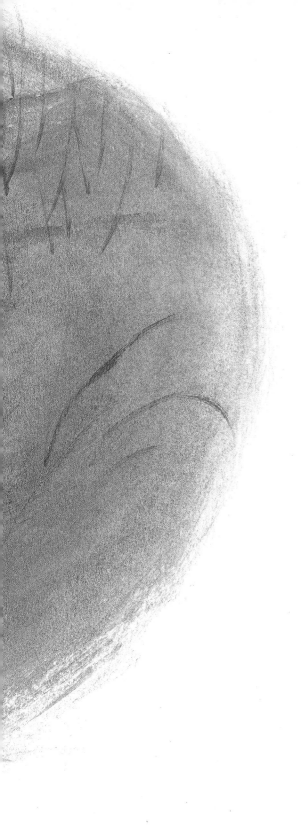

On this special island
so wild and free,
where a whole herd of ponies
lives peacefully,
a mother and foal
bed down by the sea.

AUTHOR'S NOTE

Assateague Island is a long, narrow strip of land just off the coast of both Maryland and Virginia. It is one of my favorite places. Every time I visit, I learn more about its many shore and marsh-dwelling birds. I find places where the island deer feed, or swim, or bed down. It is a wild and wonderful island.

The most fascinating creatures on Assateague are the wild ponies. No one seems to know how the ponies got on the island originally, but as far back as most people can remember, there have been ponies on Assateague Island.

Seeing the wild ponies on their beautiful island is a thrill. My wife Deanna and I have spent many whole days watching and videotaping the ponies and birds on the beach and in the marshes. On the day we visited Assateague to research this book, we saw ponies not only on the beach but also on the dunes and on the mudflats. And just before we left the island, we saw ponies running and splashing in the ocean surf.

I have tried to squeeze everything I love about Assateague Island and its wild inhabitants into this book. I hope it makes you love the island and want to go there someday to see it all for yourself.

Jim Arnosky

www.jimarnosky.com

FOR GREG,

who loves these wild ponies and their beautiful island.

To create his paintings, Jim Arnosky used acrylic paint applied in an oil technique.

The type is set in Veljovic Book. The title type is set in ITC Cancione, altered by the designer.

Book design by Melissa Farris

Library of Congress Cataloging-in-Publication Data

Arnosky, Jim.
Wild ponies / by Jim Arnosky.
p. cm. -- (One whole day)
Summary: Presents a day in the life of a herd of wild ponies on
Assateague Island.
ISBN 0-7922-7121-1 (hardcover)
1. Chincoteague pony--Assateague Island (Md. and Va.)--Juvenile
literature. 2. Wild ponies--Assateague Island (Md. and Va.)--Juvenile
literature. [1. Chincoteague pony. 2. Ponies. 3. Assateague Island
(Md. and Va.)] I. Title. II. Series.
SF315.2.C4 A75 2002
636.1'6--dc21
2001008626

Printed in Belgium

One of the world's largest nonprofit scientific and educational organizations, the National Geographic Society was founded in 1888 "for the increase and diffusion of geographic knowl-edge." Fulfilling this mission, the Society educates and inspires millions every day through its magazines, books, television programs, videos, maps and atlases, research grants, the National Geographic Bee, teacher workshops, and innovative classroom materials. The Society is supported through membership dues, charitable gifts, and income from the sale of its educational products. This support is vital to National Geographic's mission to increase global understanding and promote conservation of our planet through exploration, research, and education.

For more information, please call 1-800-NGS LINE (647-5463) or write to the following address:

National Geographic Society
1145 17th Street N.W.
Washington, D.C. 20036-4688 U.S.A.
Visit the Society's Web site: www.nationalgeographic.com

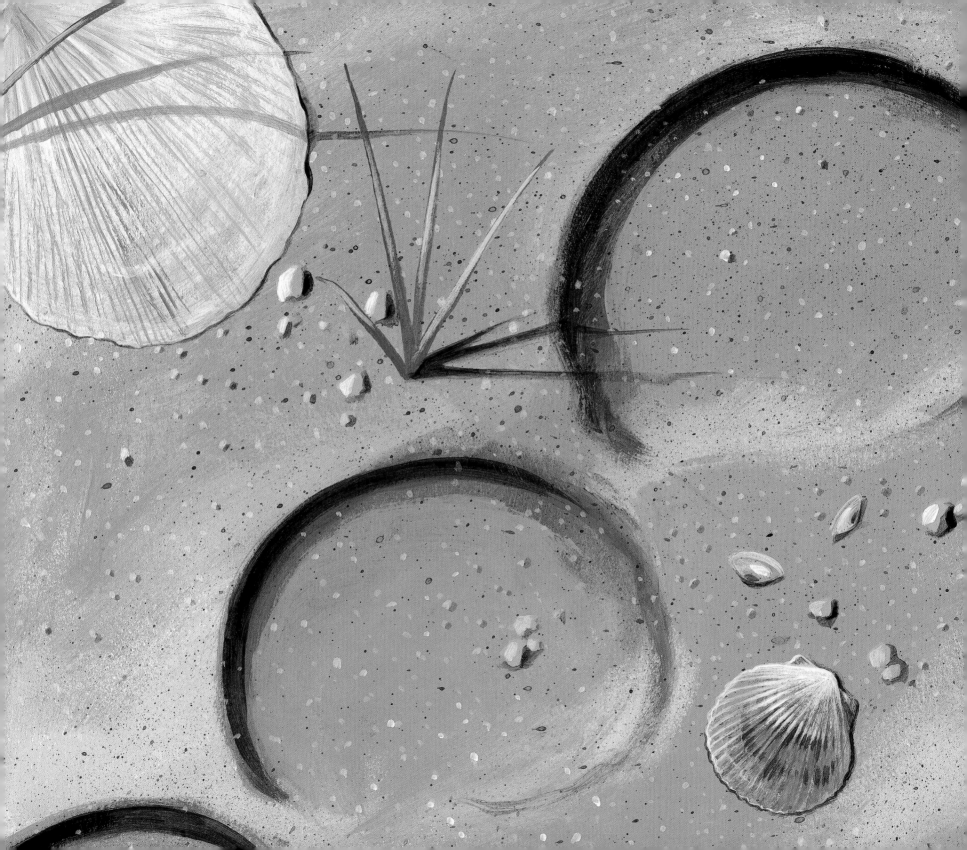